easy meals

sizzling dishes

p

This is a Parragon Publishing Book
This edition published in 2004

Parragon Publishing
Queen Street House
4 Queen Street
Bath BA1 1HE, UK

ISBN: 1-40541-512-6

Printed in China

Produced by The Bridgewater Book Company Ltd, Lewes, East Sussex

Creative Director Terry Jeavons
Art Director Sarah Howerd
Page Make-up Sara Kidd
Editorial Director Fiona Biggs
Senior Editor Mark Truman
Editorial Assistant Tom Kitch

NOTES FOR THE READER

- This book uses both metric and US measurements. Follow the same units of measurement throughout; do not mix metric and US measurements.
- All spoon measurements are level: teaspoons are assumed to be 5 ml, and table-spoons are assumed to be 15 ml.
- Cup measurements in this book are for American cups.
- Unless otherwise stated, milk is assumed to be whole milk, eggs and individual vegetables such as potatoes are medium-sized, and pepper is freshly ground black pepper.
- Recipes using raw or very lightly cooked eggs should be avoided by infants, the elderly, pregnant women, convalescents, and anyone suffering from an illness.
- Optional ingredients, variations, and serving suggestions have not been included in the calculations.
- The times given are an approximate guide only. Preparation times differ according to the techniques used by different people and the cooking times vary as a result of the type of oven used.

Contents

Introduction

If your busy life-style leaves you with little spare time for cooking, but you are finding your usual recipes for fast food rather bland and boring, the recipes in this book will be a revelation. Your senses will really sit up and take notice when you present them with these sizzling hot and spicy dishes, bursting with mouthwatering flavors and enticing aromas.

The recipes have been specifically selected because they are easy to prepare and cook, so now even your mid-week meals can be exciting and different. Many of the ingredients can be kept on hand in the pantry; all you need to do is add fresh fish, or meat, or vegetables to create something quite out-of-the-ordinary. The dishes are gathered from a variety of cultures around the world, including Thai, Mexican, and Chinese, and they reflect today's changing attitudes to eating: less heavy and

guide to recipe key	
easy	Recipes are graded as follows: 1 pea = easy; 2 peas = very easy; 3 peas = extremely easy.
serves 4	Most of the recipes in this book serve four people. Simply halve the ingredients to serve two, taking care not to mix US and metric measurements.
15 minutes	Preparation time. Where recipes include marinating, soaking, standing, or chilling, times for these are listed separately: eg, 15 minutes, plus 30 minutes to marinate.
15 minutes	Cooking time. Cooking times do not include the cooking of rice or noodles served with the main dishes.

conventional, more adventurous and fun. Many of the dishes are quickly stir-fried or are broiled, so they are even ideal for weight-watchers and the health-conscious.

And if you enjoy entertaining but find yourself with little time to prepare lavish meals, you will find plenty of recipes in this book to help you out. A simple menu such as Lemon Grass Chicken Skewers followed by Thai-Spiced Salmon, with an Exotic Fruit Salad for dessert, looks and tastes impressive and takes little time to assemble and cook, enabling you to unwind with your guests on any day of the week.

Fish Tacos, page 60

Soups, Appetizers & Light Dishes

This first part of the book is full of ideas for soups and other first-course dishes which would also make a light lunch or a one-dish supper. Chicken, Avocado & Chipotle Soup includes all the classic ingredients of Mexican cooking. Hot and Sour Noodles is a Thai snack, served all day long from market stalls in Thailand. Red Rice Salad with Hot Dressing is just one spicy alternative for vegetarians who like a sizzle to their suppers.

Parsnip Soup with Ginger & Orange

INGREDIENTS

2 tsp olive oil
1 large onion, chopped
1 large leek, sliced
1lb 12 oz/800 g
   parsnips, sliced
2 carrots, sliced thinly
4 tbsp grated, peeled
   fresh ginger
2–3 garlic cloves,
   chopped finely
grated zest of ½ orange
6 cups water
salt and pepper
1 cup orange juice
snipped chives or slivers
   of scallions, to
   garnish

very easy

serves 6

15 minutes

50 minutes

VARIATION
The soup may be made using equal amounts (1 lb/450 g each) of carrots and parsnips.

❶ Heat the olive oil in a large pan over a medium heat. Add the onion and leek and cook for about 5 minutes, stirring occasionally, until softened,

❷ Add the parsnips, carrots, ginger, garlic, grated orange zest, water, and a large pinch of salt. Reduce the heat, cover, and simmer for about 40 minutes, stirring occasionally, until the vegetables are very soft.

❸ Allow the soup to cool slightly, then transfer to a blender or a food processor and blend until smooth, working in batches if necessary. (If using a food processor, strain off the cooking liquid and reserve. Purée the soup solids with enough cooking liquid to moisten them, then combine with the remaining liquid.)

❹ Return the soup to the pan and stir in the orange juice. Add a little water or more orange juice if you prefer a thinner consistency. Taste and, if necessary, adjust the seasoning with salt and pepper

❺ Simmer the soup for about 10 minutes to heat it through. Ladle the hot soup into warm soup bowls, and serve immediately, garnished with chives or slivers of scallions, and serve.

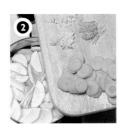

Spicy Lamb Soup with Garbanzos & Zucchinis

INGREDIENTS

1–2 tbsp olive oil
1 lb/450 g lean boneless
   lamb, such as
   shoulder or neck fillet,
   trimmed of fat and cut
   into ½ inch/1 cm cubes
1 onion, chopped finely
2–3 garlic cloves, crushed
5 cups water
14 oz/400 g can chopped
   tomatoes in juice
1 bay leaf
½ tsp dried thyme
½ tsp dried oregano
⅛ tsp ground cinnamon
¼ tsp ground cumin
¼ tsp ground turmeric
1 tsp harissa
14 oz can garbanzos,
   rinsed and drained
1 carrot, diced
1 potato, diced
1 zucchini, quartered
   lengthwise and sliced
3½ oz/100 g fresh or
   defrosted frozen green
   peas
chopped fresh mint or
   cilantro, to garnish

❶ Heat the oil in a large pan or cast-iron casserole over a medium–high heat. Add the lamb, in batches if necessary to avoid crowding the pan, and cook until evenly browned on all sides, adding a little more oil if needed. Remove the meat with a slotted spoon when browned.

❷ Reduce the heat and add the onion and garlic to the pan. Cook, stirring frequently, for 1–2 minutes.

❸ Add the water and return all the meat to the pan. Bring just to a boil and skim off any foam that rises to the surface. Reduce the heat and stir in the tomatoes, bay leaf, thyme, oregano, cinnamon, cumin, turmeric, and harissa. Simmer for about 1 hour, or until the meat is very tender. Discard the bay leaf.

❹ Stir in the garbanzos, carrot and potato and simmer for 15 minutes. Add the zucchini and peas and continue simmering for 15–20 minutes, or until all the vegetables are tender.

❺ Adjust the seasoning, adding more harissa, if desired. Ladle the soup into warm bowls, and garnish with mint or cilantro before serving.

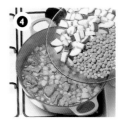

very easy

serves 4–5

20 minutes

1 hour 45 minutes

Spicy Gazpacho

very easy

serves 4–6

30 minutes,
plus a few hours
to chill

0 minutes

❶ Peel the cucumber, cut it in half lengthwise, then cut into quarters. Remove the seeds with a teaspoon and dice the flesh. Cut the peppers in half, remove the cores and seeds, then dice the flesh. Deseed and chop the chile.

❷ If you prefer to skin the tomatoes, place in a heatproof bowl, pour boiling water over to cover them, and let stand for 30 seconds. Drain and plunge into cold water. The skins will then slide off easily. Cut the tomatoes in half, deseed if you prefer, then chop the flesh.

❸ Combine half the cucumber, bell peppers, tomatoes and onion in a blender or a food processor with all the chile, garlic, olive oil, cumin, vinegar, cilantro, and parsley. Process these ingredients with enough of the tomato juice to make a smooth purée.

❹ Pour the puréed soup into a bowl and stir in the remaining bell peppers, cucumber, tomatoes and onion. Season with salt and pepper to taste, then cover and chill in the refrigerator for a few hours.

❺ To serve, stir, ladle the gazpacho into soup bowls, and add 1–2 ice cubes to each portion.

Chicken, Avocado, & Chipotle Soup

INGREDIENTS

6 cups chicken bouillon
2–3 garlic cloves
1–2 chipotle chilis, cut into very thin strips
1 avocado
lime or lemon juice, for tossing
3–5 scallions, sliced thinly
12–14 oz/350–400 g cooked chicken breast meat, torn or cut into shreds or thin strips
2 tbsp chopped fresh cilantro

TO SERVE
1 lime, cut into wedges
handful of tortilla chips

 extremely easy

 serves 4

 15 minutes

 20 minutes

❶ Place the bouillon in a pan with the garlic and chipotle chilis and bring to a boil.

❷ Meanwhile, cut the avocado in half around the pit. Twist apart, then remove the pit with a knife. Carefully peel off the skin, dice the flesh, and toss in lime or lemon juice to prevent discoloration.

❸ Arrange the scallions, chicken, avocado, and fresh cilantro in the base of 4 soup bowls or in a serving bowl.

❹ Ladle the hot soup directly into the bowls, and serve, garnishing each bowl with lime wedges and a handful of tortilla chips, if using.

COOK'S TIP

Chipotle chilis are smoked, dried jalapeño chilis. They are very hot. If possible, use chipotles canned in adobo marinade for this recipe.

Hot & Sour Soup

INGREDIENTS

*12 oz/350 g whole raw
or cooked jumbo
shrimp in shells*
1 tbsp vegetable oil
*1 lemon grass stem,
chopped roughly*
*2 kaffir lime leaves,
shredded*
*1 green chile, deseeded
and chopped*
*5 cups chicken or fish
bouillon*
1 lime
1 tbsp Thai fish sauce
salt and pepper
*1 red bird's eye chile,
deseeded and sliced*
1 scallion, sliced thinly
*1 tbsp chopped cilantro,
to garnish*

very easy

serves 4

20 minutes

30 minutes

❶ Peel and devein the shrimp, then cover and chill until needed. Reserve the shells.

❷ Heat the oil in a large pan and stir-fry the shrimp shells for 3–4 minutes until they turn pink. Add the lemon grass, lime leaves, chile and bouillon. Pare a strip of zest from the lime and add to the pan.

❸ Bring to a boil, then lower the heat, cover, and simmer for about 20 minutes.

❹ Strain the liquid and pour it back into the pan. Squeeze the juice from the lime and add to the pan with the fish sauce and salt and pepper to taste.

❺ Return to a boil, then lower the heat, add the shrimp, and simmer for 2–3 minutes.

❻ Add the thinly sliced red bird's eye chile and scallion. Sprinkle with cilantro and serve.

COOK'S TIP

To devein the shrimp, remove the shells. Cut a slit along the back and remove the fine black vein that runs along the length of the back. Wipe the shrimp with paper towels.

Roasted Spare Ribs with Honey & Soy

INGREDIENTS

2 lb 4 oz/1 kg Chinese-
    style spare ribs
½ lemon
½ small orange
1 in/2.5 cm piece fresh
    ginger, peeled
2 garlic cloves, peeled
1 small onion, chopped
2 tbsp soy sauce
2 tbsp rice wine
½ tsp Thai 7-spice
    powder
2 tbsp honey
1 tbsp sesame oil

 very easy

 serves 4

 15 minutes

1 hour
10 minutes

❶ Place the ribs in a wide roasting pan, cover loosely with foil and cook in an oven preheated to 350°F/180°C for 30 minutes.

❷ Meanwhile, remove any seeds from the lemon and orange, and place the fruit in a food processor with the ginger, garlic, onion, soy sauce, rice wine, 7-spice powder, honey, and sesame oil. Process until smooth.

❸ Pour off any fat from the spare ribs, then spoon the puréed mixture over them. Toss the ribs to coat evenly.

❹ Return the ribs to the oven at 400° F/200°C and roast for about 40 minutes, turning and basting them occasionally, or until golden brown. Serve hot.

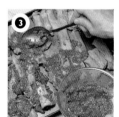

COOK'S TIP
If you do not have a food processor, grate the zest and squeeze the juice from the citrus fruits, grate the ginger, crush the garlic, and chop the onion finely. Mix together with the remaining ingredients.

Lemon Grass Chicken Skewers

INGREDIENTS

2 long or 4 short lemon
grass stems
2 large boneless,
skinless chicken
breasts, about 14 oz/
400 g in total
1 small egg white
1 carrot, grated finely
1 small red chile,
deseeded and
chopped
2 tbsp chopped fresh
garlic chives
2 tbsp chopped fresh
cilantro
1 tbsp sunflower oil
salt and pepper
cilantro and lime slices,
to garnish

 very easy

 serves 4

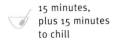 15 minutes,
plus 15 minutes
to chill

4–6 minutes

❶ If the lemon grass stems are long, cut them in half across the middle to make 4 short lengths. Cut each stalk in half lengthwise, so you have 8 sticks.

❷ Roughly chop the chicken pieces and place them in a food processor with the egg white. Process to a smooth paste, then add the carrot, chile, chives, cilantro, and salt and pepper. Process for a few seconds to mix well.

❸ Chill the mixture in the refrigerator for about 15 minutes. Divide the mixture into 8 equal portions, then with your hands, shape each portion round a skewer of lemon grass.

❹ Brush the skewers with sunflower oil, and broil under a preheated medium–hot broiler for 4–6 minutes, turning occasionally, until cooked or, grill over medium-hot coals.

❺ Serve the chicken skewers hot, with cilantro and slices of lime to garnish.

COOK'S TIP

If you cannot buy whole lemon grass stems, use wooden or bamboo skewers instead, and add ½ teaspoon ground lemon grass to the mixture with the other flavorings.

Beef Satay with Groundnut Sauce

1 lb 2 oz/500 g beef
  tenderloin
2 garlic cloves, crushed
3/4 inch/8 mm piece
  fresh ginger, grated
  finely
1 tbsp soft light brown
  sugar
1 tbsp dark soy sauce
1 tbsp lime juice
2 tsp sesame oil
1 tsp ground coriander
1 tsp turmeric
1/2 tsp chili powder
crisp salad, to serve

GROUNDNUT SAUCE
8 tbsp crunchy
  groundnut butter
1/2 small onion, grated
1 1/4 cups coconut milk
2 tsp brown sugar
1/2 tsp chili powder
1 tbsp dark soy sauce

 very easy

 serves 4

 10 minutes, plus 2
  hours to marinate

 3–5 minutes

❶ Cut the beef into 1/2 inch/1 cm cubes.

❷ Place the beef cubes in a large bowl and add the garlic, ginger, sugar, soy sauce, lime juice, sesame oil, ground coriander, turmeric, and chili powder. Mix well to coat the pieces of meat evenly. Cover and leave to marinate in the refrigerator for at least 2 hours, or overnight.

❸ To make the groundnut sauce, place all the ingredients in a pan and stir over a medium heat until they boil. Remove from the heat and keep warm.

❹ Thread the beef cubes onto bamboo skewers. Broil under a preheated broiler for 3–5 minutes, turning often, until golden. Alternatively, barbecue over hot coals. Serve with the sauce and a crisp salad.

COOK'S TIP
Soak the skewers in cold water for about 20 minutes before threading the meat onto them to reduce the risk of the skewers burning on the grill.

Hot & Sour Noodles

INGREDIENTS

9 oz/250 g dried
   medium egg noodles
1 tbsp sesame oil
1 tbsp chili oil
1 garlic clove, crushed
2 scallions, chopped
   finely
⅔ cup button
   mushrooms, sliced
1 cup dried Chinese
   black mushrooms,
   soaked, drained, and
   sliced
2 tbsp lime juice
3 tbsp light soy sauce
1 tsp sugar

TO SERVE
shredded Chinese
   cabbage
2 tbsp chopped cilantro
2 tbsp toasted peanuts

 extremely easy

 serves 4

 10 minutes,
   2 hours to soak

 15 minutes

❶ Cook the noodles in a large pan of boiling water for 3–4 minutes, or according to the package directions. Drain well, then toss with the sesame oil and set aside.

❷ Heat the chili oil in a large wok and quickly stir-fry the garlic, scallions, and button mushrooms until softened.

❸ Add the black mushrooms, lime juice, soy sauce, and sugar and continue stir-frying until the mushrooms are cooked. Add the noodles and toss to mix. Spoon the mixture over the Chinese cabbage, sprinkled with chopped cilantro and peanuts, and serve.

COOK'S TIP
Thai chili oil is very hot, so if you want a milder flavor use vegetable oil to cook, and dribble a little chili oil over the noodles as a seasoning just before serving.

Roasted Cheese with Salsa

INGREDIENTS

8 oz/225 g mozzarella, fresh pecorino or Mexican queso Oaxaca

²⁄₃ cup tomato salsa, or other good salsa

½ onion, chopped finely

8 soft corn tortillas, to serve

extremely easy

serves 4

5 minutes

20 minutes

❶ To warm the corn tortillas ready for serving, heat a nonstick skillet, add a tortilla, and sprinkle it with a few drops of water as it heats. Wrap it in aluminum foil to keep it warm. Repeat the same process with each of the remaining tortillas.

❷ Cut chunks or slabs of the cheese and arrange in a shallow ovenproof dish or in individual dishes.

❸ Spoon the salsa over the cheese, covering it, and place in a preheated oven at 400°F/200°C, or under a preheated broiler. Cook until the cheese melts and bubbles, browning a little in spots.

❹ Sprinkle with chopped onion to taste and serve with the warmed tortillas for dipping. Serve the dish immediately, because the melted cheese turns stringy when it is cold, and becomes difficult to eat.

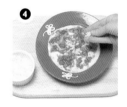

Shrimp Satay

INGREDIENTS

12 peeled raw jumbo
shrimp

MARINADE
1 tsp ground coriander
1 tsp ground cumin
2 tbsp light soy sauce
4 tbsp vegetable oil
1 tbsp curry powder
1 tbsp ground turmeric
½ cup coconut milk
3 tbsp sugar

PEANUT SAUCE
2 tbsp vegetable oil
3 garlic cloves, crushed
1 tbsp red curry paste
½ cup coconut milk
1 cup fish or chicken
bouillon
1 tbsp sugar
1 tsp salt
1 tbsp lemon juice
4 tbsp unsalted roasted
peanuts, chopped
finely
4 tbsp dried bread
crumbs

❶ Slit the shrimp down their backs and remove the black vein, if any. Set aside. Mix together the marinade ingredients and add the shrimp. Stir well, cover, and set aside for at least 8 hours, or overnight.

❷ To make the peanut sauce, heat the oil in a large skillet until very hot. Add the garlic and cook until it starts to color. Add the curry paste and mix, cooking for 30 seconds longer. Add the coconut milk, bouillon, sugar, salt, and lemon juice, stirring. Bring to a boil and cook for 1–2 minutes, stirring constantly. Add the peanuts and bread crumbs, and mix together well. Pour the sauce into a bowl and set aside.

❸ Using 4 skewers, thread 3 shrimp onto each. Cook under a preheated hot broiler or on the barbecue for 3–4 minutes on each side until just cooked through. Serve immediately with the peanut sauce.

❶  ❷  ❸

 very easy

 serves 4

 20 minutes,
plus 8 hours
to marinate

 15 minutes

Thai Fish Cakes with Sweet & Sour Chili Dipping Sauce

1 lb/450 g firm white
fish, such as hake,
haddock, or cod,
skinned and chopped
roughly
1 tbsp Thai fish sauce
1 tbsp red curry paste
1 kaffir lime leaf,
shredded finely
2 tbsp chopped cilantro
1 egg
1 tsp brown sugar
large pinch salt
1½ oz/40 g green
beans, thinly
sliced crosswise
vegetable oil, for pan-
frying

SWEET & SOUR
DIPPING SAUCE
4 tbsp sugar
1 tbsp cold water
3 tbsp white rice
vinegar
2 small, hot chiles,
chopped finely
1 tbsp fish sauce

❶ To make the fish cakes, put the fish, fish sauce, curry paste, lime leaf, cilantro, egg, sugar, and salt into the bowl of a food processor. Process until smooth. Scrape into a bowl and stir in the green beans. Set aside.

❷ To make the dipping sauce, put the sugar, water, and rice vinegar into a small pan, and heat gently until all the sugar has dissolved. Bring to a boil and simmer for 2 minutes. Remove the pan from the heat, and stir in the chiles and fish sauce, and let stand to cool.

❸ Pour enough oil into a skillet to cover the bottom generously, and heat. Divide the fish mixture into 16 little balls. Flatten the balls into little patties and cook in the hot oil for 1–2 minutes each side until golden. Drain on paper towels. Serve the fish cakes with the dipping sauce.

 very easy

 serves 4

 15 minutes

 6–8 minutes

Meat

Beef, lamb, pork, and chicken all work well in sizzling, spicy dishes. Red-Hot Beef with Cashews can be prepared well in advance of a mealtime, and finished off quickly when ready to serve. Chicken & Mango Stir-Fry is a healthy dish with an exciting blend of textures: spicy chicken, crisp vegetables, and smooth, sweet mango. It takes just over 30 minutes from preparation to serving. This section contains unusual dishes, such as Mumbar from the Persian Gulf, an exotically seasoned lamb sausage.

Red-Hot Beef with Cashews

1 lb 2 oz/500 g
  boneless, lean beef
  sirloin, sliced thinly
1 tsp. vegetable oil

MARINADE
1 tbsp sesame seeds
1 garlic clove, chopped
1 tbsp fresh ginger,
  chopped finely
1 red bird's eye chile,
  chopped
2 tbsp dark soy sauce
1 tsp. red curry paste

TO FINISH
1 tsp sesame oil
4 tbsp unsalted cashew
  nuts
1 scallion, sliced thickly
  on the diagonal

❶ Cut the beef into strips ½ inch/1 cm wide. Place them in a large, nonmetal bowl.

❷ To make the marinade, toast the sesame seeds in a heavy-based pan over a medium heat for 2–3 minutes until golden brown, shaking the pan occasionally.

❸ Place the seeds in a mortar with the garlic, ginger, and chile, and grind with a pestle to a smooth paste. Add the soy sauce and curry paste, and mix well.

❹ Spoon the paste over the beef strips, and toss well to coat the meat evenly. Cover and leave to marinate in the refrigerator for 2–3 hours, or overnight.

❺ Heat a large griddle or a heavy skillet until very hot and brush with vegetable oil. Place the beef strips on it and cook quickly, turning often, until lightly browned. Remove from the heat and spoon into a pile on a hot serving dish.

❻ Heat the sesame oil in a small pan and quickly cook the cashew nuts until they are golden. Add the scallions and stir-fry for 30 seconds. Sprinkle the mixture over the beef strips, and serve immediately.

 very easy

 serves 4

 20 minutes,
plus 2–3 hours
to marinate

 15 minutes

Red Lamb Curry

1 lb 2 oz/500 g boneless
   lean leg of lamb
2 tbsp vegetable oil
1 large onion, sliced
2 garlic cloves, crushed
2 tbsp Thai red curry
   paste
²⁄₃ cup coconut milk
1 tbsp soft light brown
   sugar
1 large red bell pepper,
   deseeded and sliced
   thickly
½ cup beef (or lamb)
   bouillon
1 tbsp Thai fish sauce
2 tbsp lime juice
8 oz/225 g can water
   chestnuts, drained
2 tbsp chopped fresh
   cilantro
2 tbsp chopped fresh
   basil
salt and pepper
boiled jasmine rice,
   to serve

❶ Trim the meat and cut it into 1¼/3 cm inch cubes. Heat the oil in a wok over a high heat and stir-fry the onion and garlic for 2–3 minutes to soften. Add the meat cubes and cook quickly until lightly browned.

❷ Stir in the curry paste and cook for a few seconds, then add the coconut milk and sugar, and bring to a boil. Reduce the heat and simmer for 15 minutes, stirring occasionally.

❸ Stir in the red bell pepper, and the bouillon, fish sauce, and lime juice, cover, and continue simmering for an additional 15 minutes, or until the meat is tender.

❹ Add the water chestnuts, cilantro, and basil, then adjust the seasoning to taste. Serve with jasmine rice.

very easy

serves 4

20 minutes

45–50 minutes

Chicken & Mango Stir-Fry

*6 boneless, skinless
  chicken thighs
1 inch/2.5 cm piece fresh
  ginger, grated
1 garlic clove, crushed
1 small red chile,
  deseeded
1 large red bell pepper
4 scallions
1½ cups snow peas
1 cup baby corn
1 large, ripe mango
2 tbsp sunflower oil
1 tbsp light soy sauce
3 tbsp rice wine,
  or dry sherry
1 tsp sesame oil
salt and pepper
sliced chives, to garnish*

❶ Cut the chicken into long, thin strips and place in a bowl. Mix together the ginger, garlic, and chile, then stir into the chicken strips to coat them evenly.

❷ Slice the bell pepper thinly, cutting diagonally. Trim and scallions and slice them diagonally, and cut the snow peas and corn in half diagonally. Peel the mango, remove the pit, and slice the fruit thinly.

❸ Heat the oil in a wok or a large skillet over a high heat. Add the chicken and stir-fry for 4–5 minutes until it just turns golden brown. Add the bell peppers and stir-fry over a medium heat for 4–5 minutes to soften. Add the scallions, corn, and snow peas, and stir-fry for an additional minute.

❹ Mix together the soy sauce, rice wine or sherry, and sesame oil and stir it into the wok. Add the mango and stir gently for 1 minute to heat thoroughly. Adjust the seasoning with salt and pepper to taste, and serve immediately.

 very easy

 serves 4

 20 minutes

 15 minutes

Thai-Spiced Cilantro Chicken

INGREDIENTS

4 boneless chicken
breasts, without skin

MARINADE
2 garlic cloves, peeled
1 fresh green chile,
   deseeded
¾ in/2 cm piece fresh
   ginger, peeled
4 tbsp chopped fresh
   cilantro
finely grated zest of 1
   lime
3 tbsp lime juice
2 tbsp light soy sauce
1 tbsp superfine sugar
¾ cup coconut milk

❶ Using a sharp knife, cut 3 deep slashes into the skinned side of each chicken breast. Place the breasts in a single layer in a wide, nonmetal dish.

❷ Put the garlic, chili, ginger, cilantro, lime zest, and juice, soy sauce, superfine sugar, and coconut milk in a food processor, and process until a smooth purée forms.

❸ Spread the purée over both sides of the chicken breasts, coating them evenly. Cover the dish and leave to marinate in the refrigerator for about 1 hour.

❹ Lift the chicken from the marinade, drain off the excess, and place in a broiler pan. Broil under a preheated broiler for 12–15 minutes until cooked thoroughly and evenly.

❺ Meanwhile, put the remaining marinade in a pan, and bring to a boil. Lower the heat and simmer for several minutes to heat thoroughly. Serve with the chicken breasts.

 very easy

 serves 4

 15 minutes, plus 1 hour to marinate

 15–20 minutes

Duck Breasts with Chili & Lime

MARINADE
2 garlic cloves, crushed
4 tsp brown sugar
3 tbsp lime juice
1 tbsp soy sauce
1 tsp chili sauce

4 boneless duck breasts
1 tsp vegetable oil
½ cup chicken bouillon
2 tbsp plum jam
salt and pepper

❶ Mix together the garlic, sugar, lime juice, and soy and chili sauces.

❷ Using a small sharp knife, cut deep slashes in the skin of the duck to make a diamond pattern. Place the duck breasts in a wide, nonmetal dish.

❸ Spoon the mixture over the duck breasts, turning to coat them evenly. Cover the dish with plastic wrap and let marinate in the refrigerator for at least 3 hours, or overnight.

❹ Drain the duck, reserving the marinade. Heat a large, heavy-based pan until very hot and brush with the oil. Add the duck breasts, skin side down, and cook for 4–5 minutes until the skin is browned and crisp. Pour off the excess fat.

❺ Turn the duck breasts and cook on the other side for 2–3 minutes to brown. Add the reserved marinade, jam, and bouillon, and simmer for 2 minutes. Adjust the seasoning to taste and serve hot, with the juices spooned over the meat.

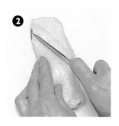

easy

serves 4

15 minutes,
plus 3 hours
to marinate

10 minutes

Drunken Noodles

6 oz/175 g rice noodles
2 tbsp vegetable oil
1 garlic clove, crushed
2 small green chiles,
    chopped
1 small onion, sliced
    thinly
5½ oz/150 g lean ground
    pork or chicken
1 small green bell
    pepper, deseeded and
    chopped finely
4 kaffir lime leaves,
    shredded finely
1 tbsp dark soy sauce
1 tbsp light soy sauce
½ tsp sugar
1 tomato, cut into thin
    wedges
2 tbsp sweet basil leaves

❶ Soak the rice noodles in hot water for 15 minutes, or according to the package directions. Drain well.

❷ Heat the oil in a wok and stir-fry the garlic, chiles, and onion for 1 minute. Stir in the pork or chicken, and stir-fry on a high heat for an additional minute. Add the bell pepper and continue stir-frying for an additional 2 minutes or so.

❸ Stir in the lime leaves, soy sauces, and sugar. Add the rice noodles and tomato, and toss well to heat thoroughly.

❹ Sprinkle with chopped basil and serve hot.

 very easy

 serves 4

 10 minutes,
plus 15 minutes
to soak noodles

 5 minutes

COOK'S TIP
Fresh kaffir lime leaves freeze well. If you buy more than you need, tie them in a tightly sealed plastic freezer bag and freeze them for up to a month. They can be used from the freezer.

Mumbar

BAHARAT SEASONING
MIX
2 tbsp black peppercorns
1 tbsp coriander seeds
2 tsp whole cloves
1½ tsp cumin seeds
1 tsp cardamom seeds
1 cinnamon stick, broken
    into small pieces
1 whole nutmeg
2 tbsp hot paprika

½ cup basmati rice
2 lb/900 lb ground lamb
1 small onion, chopped
    finely
3–4 garlic cloves, crushed
1 bunch each flatleaf
    parsley and cilantro,
    chopped finely
2–3 tbsp tomato ketchup
1 tbsp vegetable oil
pared rind and juice of 1
    lime
3 cups hot lamb bouillon
salt and pepper

❶ To make the baharat seasoning, grind the first 6 ingredients into a fine powder. Grate the whole nutmeg into the mix and stir in the paprika. Store in an airtight jar.

❷ Bring a pan of salted water to a boil. Pour in the rice, return to a boil, then simmer until the rice is tender, but firm to the bite. Drain and rinse.

❸ Place the lamb in a large bowl and break up with a fork. Add the onion, garlic, parsley, cilantro, ketchup, and 1 teaspoon of the baharat. Stir in the cooked rice and season. Squeeze the mixture to make it pastelike.

❹ Divide into 4–6 pieces and roll each into a sausage 1 inch/ 2.5 cm thick. Brush a 9–10 inch/23–25 cm skillet with the oil. Starting in the center of the pan, coil the sausage pieces, joining each piece, to form one long coiled sausage.

❺ Press lightly to make an even layer, then tuck the lime zest into the coils of the sausage. Pour the lime juice and hot bouillon into the pan, and cover with a heatproof plate.

❻ Bring to a boil, then simmer gently for about 10 minutes. Cover, continue to cook for 15 minutes, and remove from the heat. Drain, and slide the sausage onto a serving plate. Sprinkle with a little more of the baharat to serve.

easy

serves 6–8

30 minutes

25 minutes

Red Pork Curry with Jasmine-Scented Rice

INGREDIENTS

RED CURRY PASTE
1 tbsp coriander seeds
2 tsp cumin seeds
2 tsp black or white
    peppercorns
1 tsp salt, or to taste
5–8 dried hot red chilis
3–4 shallots, chopped
6–8 garlic cloves
2-inch piece fresh
    ginger root, chopped
2 tsp kaffir lime zest or
    or leaves, shredded
1 tbsp red chili powder
1 tbsp shrimp paste
2 stalks lemon grass,
    sliced thinly

2 lb/900 g boned pork
    shoulder, cut into
    thin slices
3 cups coconut milk
2 red chiles, deseeded
    and sliced thinly
2 tbsp Thai fish sauce
2 tsp brown sugar
1 large red bell pepper,
    deseeded and sliced
6 kaffir lime leaves
½ bunch fresh mint
½ bunch Thai basil
jasmine-scented or Thai
    fragrant rice, to serve

❶ To make the red curry paste, grind the coriander seeds, cumin seeds, peppercorns, and salt to a fine powder. Add the chiles, one by one, according to taste, until ground.

❷ Put the shallots, ginger root, kaffir lime zest or leaves, chili powder, and shrimp paste in a food processor. Process for about 1 minute. Add the ground spices and process again. Adding water, a few drops at a time, continue to process until a thick paste forms. Scrape into a bowl and stir in the lemon grass.

❸ Put about half the red curry paste with the pork in a large, deep, heavy-based skillet with the pork. Cook over a medium heat for 2–3 minutes, stirring gently, until the pork is evenly coated and begins to brown.

❹ Stir in the coconut milk and bring to a boil. Cook, stirring frequently, for about 10 minutes. Reduce the heat, stir in the chiles, Thai fish sauce, and brown sugar, and simmer for about 20 minutes. Add the red bell pepper and simmer for 10 minutes more.

❺ Shred the lime leaves, mint, and basil, and add them to the curry. Transfer to a serving dish, sprinkle with the remaining mint and basil, and serve the dish with the rice.

easy

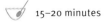
serves 4–6

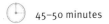
15–20 minutes

⏱ 45–50 minutes

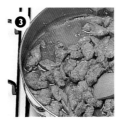

Fish & Seafood

Some people love the taste of ultra-fresh fish and shellfish. Others fail to appreciate their delicate flavors, but cook them regularly because they are a first-class low-fat, high-protein food. Whichever type you are, you will find recipes in these pages to enhance your enjoyment of fish and shellfish from river and sea. Spicy flavorings and fast sizzling will transform them. Fish Tacos are made from white fish sprinkled with spices, fried until golden, and served in a soft corn tortilla with a crisp cabbage salad. And Moroccan Fish Tagine partners red mullet with a spicy tomato sauce.

Steamed Yellow Fish

INGREDIENTS

1 lb 2 oz/500 g firm fish
fillets, such as red
snapper, sole, or
monkfish
1 dried red bird's eye chili
1 small onion, chopped
3 garlic cloves, chopped
2 sprigs fresh cilantro
1 tsp coriander seeds
½ tsp turmeric
½ tsp ground black
pepper
1 tbsp Thai fish sauce
2 tbsp coconut milk
1 small egg, beaten
2 tbsp rice flour
soy sauce, to serve

 very easy

 serves 4

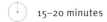 20 minutes

15–20 minutes

❶ Remove any skin from the fish and cut the fillets diagonally into long, ³/₄ inch/2 cm wide strips.

❷ Place the dried chili, the onion, garlic, and cilantro, and the coriander seeds in a mortar and grind them with a pestle to a smooth paste.

❸ Add the turmeric, pepper, fish sauce, coconut milk, and beaten egg, stirring well to mix evenly.

❹ Dip the fish strips into the paste mixture, then into the rice flour to coat them lightly.

❺ Bring the water in the bottom of a steamer to a boil, then arrange the fish strips in the top of the steamer. Cover and steam for 12–15 minutes until the fish is just firm.

❻ Serve the fish with soy sauce and an accompaniment of stir-fried vegetables or salad.

COOK'S TIP

If you do not have a steamer, improvise by placing a large metal colander over a large pan of boiling water and covering it with an upturned plate to enclose the fish as it steams.

Baked Fish with Peppers, Chiles, & Basil

INGREDIENTS

handful of fresh sweet
   basil leaves
2 tbsp groundnut oil
1 lb 10 oz/750 g whole
   red snapper or sea
   bass, cleaned
2 tbsp Thai fish sauce
2 garlic cloves, crushed
1 tsp galangal or ginger,
   grated finely
2 large red chiles,
   sliced diagonally
1 yellow bell pepper,
   deseeded and diced
1 tbsp palm sugar (or
   brown sugar)
1 tbsp rice vinegar
2 tbsp water or fish
   bouillon
2 tomatoes, deseeded
   and sliced in wedges

 very easy

serves 4

 25 minutes

35–40 minutes

❶ Reserve a few fresh basil leaves for garnish and tuck the rest inside the body cavity of the fish.

❷ Heat 1 tablespoon oil in a wide skillet and cook the fish quickly, turning once, until browned. Place the fish on a large piece of aluminum foil in a roasting pan and spoon the fish sauce over it. Wrap the foil loosely round the fish and bake it in an oven preheated to 375°F/190°C for 25–30 minutes until just cooked though.

❸ Meanwhile, heat the remaining oil and pan-fry the garlic, galangal, and chiles for 30 seconds. Add the bell peppers and stir-fry for an additional 2–3 minutes to soften.

❹ Stir in the sugar, rice vinegar, and water, then add the tomatoes and bring to a boil. Remove from the heat.

❺ Remove the fish from the oven and transfer to a warmed serving plate. Add the fish juices to the pan, then spoon the sauce over the fish and scatter with the reserved basil leaves. Serve immediately.

❶ **❷**

COOK'S TIP

Large red chiles are not as hot as tiny bird's eye chiles, so you can use them more freely in dishes which require a mild spiciness.

Thai-Spiced Salmon

INGREDIENTS

SPICE MIXTURE
1-inch/2.5 cm piece fresh
    root ginger, grated
1 tsp coriander seeds,
    crushed
¼ tsp chili powder
1 tbsp lime juice
1 tsp sesame oil

4 pieces salmon fillet
    with skin about
    5½ oz/150 g each
2 tbsp vegetable oil

 very easy

serves 4

5 minutes,
plus 30 minutes
to chill

4–5 minutes

❶ Mix together the ingredients for the spice mixture: ginger, coriander, chili, lime juice, and sesame oil.

❷ Place the salmon in a wide, nonmetal plate or dish, and spoon the mixture over the flesh side of the fillets, spreading it to coat each piece of salmon evenly.

❸ Cover the dish with plastic wrap and chill the salmon in the refrigerator for 30 minutes.

❹ Heat a wide, heavy-based skillet or griddle containing the sesame oil, over a high heat. Place the salmon on the hot skillet or griddle skin side down (see Cook's Tip).

❺ Cook the salmon for 4–5 minutes, until the salmon is crusty underneath and the flesh flakes easily. Serve at once.

COOK'S TIP
Use a heavy-based pan or a solid griddle for this recipe, so the fish cooks evenly without sticking. If the fish is very thick, you may need to turn it over carefully and cook it on the other side for 2–3 minutes.

Spicy Scallops with Lime & Chile

16 large scallops
1 tbsp butter
1 tbsp vegetable oil
1 tsp crushed garlic
1 tsp grated fresh ginger
1 bunch scallions, sliced
 finely
finely grated zest of
 1 kaffir lime
1 small red chile,
 deseeded and sliced
3 tbsp kaffir lime juice
salt and pepper

TO SERVE
lime wedges
boiled rice

① Trim the scallops to remove any black intestine, then wash and pat dry with kitchen towels. Separate the corals from the white parts, then slice each white part in half horizontally, making 2 rounds.

② Heat the butter and oil in a wok. Add the garlic and ginger, and stir-fry for 1 minute, without browning. Add the scallions and stir-fry for 1 more minute.

③ Add the scallops and continue stir-frying over a high heat for 4–5 minutes. Stir in the lime zest, chile and lime juice, and cook for an additional minute.

④ Serve the scallops hot, with the juices spooned over them, accompanied by lime wedges and boiled rice.

 very easy

serves 4

10 minutes

7–8 minutes

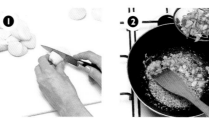

COOK'S TIP
If fresh scallops are not available, use frozen ones, but thaw them thoroughly before you cook them. Drain off all excess moisture and pat dry with kitchen towels.

Fish Tacos

INGREDIENTS

1 lb firm-fleshed white
   fish, such as red
   snapper or cod
¼ tsp dried oregano
¼ tsp ground cumin
1 tsp mild chili powder
2–3 garlic cloves,
   chopped finely
3 tbsp. all-purpose flour
vegetable oil, for frying

CABBAGE SALAD
¼ red cabbage, sliced
   finely or shredded
juice of 2 limes
hot pepper sauce or
   salsa to taste

TO FINISH
8 soft corn tortillas
1 tbsp chopped fresh
   cilantro
½ onion, chopped
   (optional)
salt and pepper
salsa of your choice

❶ Place the fish on a plate and sprinkle with half the oregano, cumin, chili powder, and garlic, and with salt and pepper, then dust with the flour.

❷ Heat the oil in a skillet until it is smoking, then cook the fish in several batches until it is golden on the outside, and just tender in the middle. Remove from the pan and place on paper towels to drain.

❸ To make the cabbage salad, combine the cabbage with the remaining oregano, cumin, chili, and garlic, then stir in the lime juice, and add salt and hot pepper sauce to taste. Set aside.

❹ Warm the tortillas one by one in an ungreased nonstick skillet, sprinkling with drops of water as they heat. As you work, wrap the tortillas in a clean dishtowel to keep them warm. Alternatively, heat in a stack in the pan, alternating the top and bottom tortillas so they warm evenly.

❺ Place some of the warm fried fish in each tortilla, with a big spoonful of the cabbage salad. Sprinkle with fresh cilantro and onion, if using. Add salsa to taste and serve the tacos at once.

easy

serves 4

15 minutes

20 minutes

Thai Crab Omelet

8 oz/225 g white crab
  meat, fresh, or
  thawed if frozen
3 scallions, chopped
  finely
1 tbsp chopped cilantro
1 tbsp chopped fresh
  chives
pinch cayenne pepper
2 tbsp vegetable oil
2 garlic cloves, crushed
1 tsp freshly grated
  ginger root
1 red chile, deseeded
  and chopped finely
2 tbsp lime juice
2 lime leaves, shredded
2 tsp sugar
2 tsp Thai fish sauce
3 eggs
4 tbsp coconut cream
1 tsp salt
scallion slivers,
  to garnish

 easy

 serves 4

10 minutes,
plus 2–3 hours
to chill

15 minutes

❶ Put the crab meat into a bowl and check that there are no small pieces of shell. Add the scallions, cilantro, chives, and cayenne, and set aside.

❷ Heat the vegetable oil and add the garlic, ginger, and chile and stir-fry for 30 seconds. Add the lime juice, lime leaves, sugar, and fish sauce. Simmer for 3–4 minutes until reduced. Remove from the heat and allow to cool. Add to the crab mixture and set aside.

❸ Beat the eggs lightly with the coconut cream and salt. In a griddle, heat the remaining vegetable oil over a medium heat. Add the egg mixture and, as it sets on the bottom, carefully pull the edges in toward the center, allowing unset egg to run underneath.

❹ When the egg is nearly set, spoon the crab mixture down the center of the omelet. Continue cooking for an additional 1–2 minutes to fin sh setting the egg, then turn the omelet out of the pan onto a serving dish. Let cool, then refrigerate the crab omelet for 2–3 hours or overnight. Cut into 4 pieces and garnish with scallion.

COOK'S TIP
You can also serve this omelette warm. After adding the crab, cook for 3–4 minutes to allow the mixture to heat through then serve immediately.

Moroccan Fish Tagine

INGREDIENTS

2 tbsp olive oil
1 large onion, chopped
large pinch saffron
½ tsp ground cinnamon
1 tsp ground coriander
½ tsp ground cumin
½ tsp ground turmeric
*7 oz/20 g can chopped
    tomatoes*
1¼ cups fish stock
*4 red mullet, cleaned,
    boned and heads and
    tails removed*
½ cup pitted green olives
*1 tbsp chopped
    preserved lemon*
*3 tbsp chopped fresh
    cilantro*
salt and pepper
couscous, to serve

❶ Heat the olive oil in a large pan or flameproof casserole. Add the onion and cook gently for 10 minutes without coloring until softened. Add the saffron, cinnamon, ground coriander, cumin, and turmeric, and cook for an additional 30 seconds, stirring.

❷ Add the chopped tomatoes and fish stock and stir well. Bring to a boil, cover and simmer for 15 minutes. Uncover and simmer for an additional 20–35 minutes until the sauce has thickened.

❸ Cut each red mullet in half then add the pieces to the pan, pushing them into the sauce. Simmer gently for an additional 5–6 minutes until the fish is just cooked.

❹ Carefully stir in the olives, preserved lemon and the chopped cilantro. Season to taste and serve with couscous.

 very easy

 serves 4

10 minutes

1 hour 15 minutes

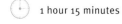

COOK'S TIP
To preserve lemons, quarter them length-wise without cutting through, pack into a preserving jar with ¼ cup sea salt per lemon, and top up with lemon juice and water to cover. Leave for at least 1 month before using.

Curried Jumbo Shrimp with Zucchinis

12 oz/350 g small
   zucchini
1 tsp salt
1 lb/450 g cooked
   jumbo shrimp
5 tbsp vegetable oil
4 garlic cloves, chopped
   finely
5 tbsp chopped cilantro
1 fresh green chile,
   deseeded and
   chopped finely
½ tsp ground turmeric
1½ tsp ground cumin
pinch cayenne pepper
7 oz/200 g can chopped
   tomatoes
1 tsp freshly grated
   ginger
1 tbsp lemon juice
steamed basmati rice,
   to serve

 very easy

serves 4

40 minutes

15–20 minutes

❶ Wash and trim the zucchini. Cut into small batons. Put into a colander and sprinkle with a little of the salt. Set aside for 30 minutes. Rinse, drain, and pat dry. Spread the shrimp on paper towels to drain.

❷ In a wok or griddle, heat the oil over a high heat. Add the garlic. As soon as the garlic begins to brown, add the zucchini, cilantro, green chili, turmeric, cumin, cayenne, tomatoes, ginger, lemon juice, and remaining salt. Stir well and bring to a boil.

❸ Cover and simmer the curry over a low heat for about 5 minutes. Uncover and add the shrimp.

❹ Increase the heat to high and simmer for about 5 minutes to reduce the liquid to a thick sauce. Serve immediately with steamed basmati rice, garnished with lime wedges.

Vegetables & Side Dishes

Exciting main dishes are often served with plain boiled rice or vegetables, yet side dishes and salads need to complement a main dish in interesting ways. If prepared with a few extra ingredients, they may take on new life. For example, horseradish brings a kick to a colorful Red Rice Salad with Hot Dressing, while a cool Thai Green Salad is enlivened with thin cucumber slices and toasted fresh coconut. Pickles are an essential accompaniment to Eastern dishes, bringing contrasting textures and tastes. Here you will find a recipe for Crisp Pickled Vegetables.

Crisp Pickled Vegetables

INGREDIENTS

½ small cauliflower
½ cucumber
2 medium carrots
7 oz/200 g green beans
½ small Chinese
    cabbage
2¼ cups rice vinegar
1 tbsp sugar
1 tsp salt

SPICE PASTE
3 garlic cloves
3 shallots
3 red bird's eye chiles
5 tbsp groundnut oil

very easy

serves 6–8

20–25 minutes

15 minutes

❶ Trim the cauliflower. Peel and deseed the cucumber. Peel the carrots. Top and tail the beans. Trim the cabbage. Cut all the vegetables into bite-sized pieces. If you have time, cut the carrots into flower shapes (see Cook's Tip).

❷ Place the rice vinegar, sugar, and salt in a large pan and bring almost to a boil. Add the vegetables, lower the heat, and simmer for 3–4 minutes until they are just tender, but still crisp inside. Remove the pan from the heat and let the vegetables and vinegar cool.

❸ To make the spice paste, peel the garlic and shallots, and deseed the chiles. Place in a mortar and grind with a pestle until a smooth paste forms.

❹ Heat the oil in a wok and stir-fry the spice paste gently for 1–2 minutes. Add the vegetables and the vinegar, and cook for an additional 2 minutes to reduce the liquid slightly. Remove from the heat and leave to cool.

❺ Serve the pickles cold, or pack into jars and store in the refrigerator for up to 2 weeks.

COOK'S TIP
To make simple carrot flowers, peel the carrot thinly as usual, then use a small sharp knife to cut narrow channels along it at regular intervals. Slice the carrot as normal, and the slices will resemble flowers.

Chile & Coconut Sambal

❶ Puncture 2 of the coconut eyes with a screwdriver, and pour the milk out from the shell. Crack the shell, prise away the flesh, and grate it coarsely into a bowl.

❷ Mix the coconut with the pineapple, onion, chiles, and lemon grass.

❸ Blend together the salt, shrimp paste, and lime juice, then stir into the sambal.

❹ Stir in the cilantro. Spoon into a small dish to serve.

 extremely easy

 serves 6–8

 15–20 minutes

0 minutes

COOK'S TIP
Grate the coconut
quickly by using a
grating blade on a
food processor.

Thai Bean Curry

INGREDIENTS

14 oz/400 g green
  beans, topped and
  tailed
1 garlic clove, sliced
  finely
1 red bird's eye chile,
  deseeded and
  chopped
½ tsp paprika pepper
1 piece lemon grass
  stalk, chopped finely
2 tsp Thai fish sauce
½ cup coconut milk
1 tbsp sunflower oil
2 scallions, sliced

❶ Cut the beans into 2 inch/5 cm pieces and cook in boiling water for 2 minutes. Drain well.

❷ Place the garlic, chile, paprika, lemon grass, fish sauce, and coconut milk in a blender, and process until a smooth paste forms.

❸ Heat the oil and stir-fry the scallions over a high heat for about 1 minute. Add the paste and bring to a boil.

❹ Simmer the mixture for 3–4 minutes to reduce the liquid by about half. Add the cooked beans to the cury, and simmer for an additional 1–2 minutes until they are tender. transfer to a serving dish and serve hot.

 very easy

serves 4

15 minutes

8–10 minutes

COOK'S TIP

Young runner beans can be used instead of green beans. Remove the strings from the beans, then cut on the diagonal into short pieces. Cook as above until tender.

Potatoes in Creamed Coconut

INGREDIENTS

1 lb 5 oz/600 g potatoes
1 onion, sliced thinly
2 red bird's eye chiles,
    chopped
½ tsp salt
½ tsp ground black
    pepper
½ cup creamed coconut
1½ cups vegetable or
    chicken stock
chopped fresh cilantro
    or basil, to garnish

❶ Peel the potatoes thinly and cut into ¾ inch chunks.

❷ Place the potatoes in a pan with the onion, chile, salt, pepper, and creamed coconut. Stir in the stock.

❸ Bring to a boil, stirring, then lower the heat, cover and simmer gently, stirring occasionally, until the potatoes are tender.

❹ Adjust the seasoning to taste, then sprinkle with chopped cilantro or basil. Serve hot.

 very easy

 serves 4

 10 minutes

 15–20 minutes

COOK'S TIP
Wash or scrub thin-skinned and new potatoes to remove any dirt, and cook them in their skins. This adds extra dietary fiber and nutrients to the dish, and cuts preparation time. Cook baby new potatoes whole.

Thai Green Salad

1 small head romaine
   lettuce
1 bunch scallions
½ cucumber
4 tbsp coarsely
   shredded fresh
   coconut, toasted

DRESSING
4 tbsp lime juice
2 tbsp Thai fish sauce
1 small bird's eye chile,
   chopped finely
1 tsp sugar
1 garlic clove, crushed
2 tbsp chopped fresh
   cilantro
1 tbsp chopped fresh
   mint

 extremely easy

 serves 4–6

 15 minutes

 0 minutes

❶ Tear the lettuce leaves or shred them roughly, and place them in a large salad bowl.

❷ Trim the scallions and slice them thinly on the diagonal, then add them to the salad bowl.

❸ Use a vegetable peeler to shave thin slices along the length of the cucumber, and add them to the salad bowl.

❹ Place all the ingredients for the dressing in a screw-top jar and shake well to mix thoroughly.

❺ Pour the dressing over the salad and toss well to coat the leaves evenly. Scatter the coconut over the salad and toss it lightly just before serving.

COOK'S TIP
To pack this salad for a picnic, put the leaves into an unbreakable salad bowl or a large plastic container, with the jar of dressing in the center. Cover with a lid or plastic wrap. The leaves stay crisp and if the dressing leaks in transit it makes no mess.

Red Rice Salad with Hot Dressing

INGREDIENTS

1 tbsp olive oil
1 cup red rice
2½ cups water
14 oz/400 g can red
   kidney beans, rinsed
   and drained
1 small red bell pepper,
   cored, deseeded, and
   diced
1 small red onion,
   chopped finely
2 small cooked beets
   (not in vinegar),
   peeled and diced
6–8 red radishes,
   sliced thinly
2–3 tbsp chopped fresh
   chives
salt and pepper
fresh chives, to garnish

HOT DRESSING
2 tbsp prepared
   horseradish
1 tbsp Dijon mustard
1 tsp sugar
¼ cup red wine vinegar
½ cup extra-virgin
   olive oil

 very easy

 serves 6–8

 15–20 minutes,
plus 1 hour
standing

 20 minutes

❶ Put the olive oil and red rice in a heavy-based pan and place over medium heat. Add the water and 1 teaspoon of salt. Bring to a boil, reduce the heat, and simmer, covered, until the rice is tender and all the water is absorbed (see Cook's Tip). Remove from the heat and allow the rice to cool to room temperature.

❷ To make the dressing, put the horseradish, mustard, and sugar in a small bowl and whisk to combine. Then gradually whisk in the vinegar, followed by the oil, to form a smooth dressing.

❸ In a large bowl, combine the red kidney beans, red bell pepper, red onion, beets, radishes, and chives, and toss together. Season with salt and pepper.

❹ Using a fork, fluff the rice into the bowl with the vegetables and toss. Pour the dressing over it and toss well. Cover and let the salad stand for about 1 hour. Spoon into a large shallow serving bowl, garnish with fresh chives, and serve immediately.

COOK'S TIP

There are several red rice varieties on the market. Read the labels carefully, as some require longer cooking than others.

Chinese Fried Rice

INGREDIENTS

2–3 tbsp groundnut or
  vegetable oil
2 onions, halved and cut
  lengthwise into thin
  wedges
2 garlic cloves, sliced
  thinly
1-inch/2.5 cm piece fresh
  ginger root, peeled,
  sliced, and cut into
  slivers
7 oz/200 g cooked ham,
  sliced thinly
4 cups cooked, cold long-
  grain white rice
9 oz/250 g cooked peeled
  shrimp
4 oz/115 g canned water
  chestnuts, sliced
3 eggs
3 tsp sesame oil

4–6 scallions, sliced on
  the diagonal into
  1-inch/2.5 cm pieces
2 tbsp dark soy or Thai
  fish sauce
1 tbsp sweet chili sauce
2 tbsp chopped fresh
  cilantro or
  flat-leaf parsley
salt and pepper

❶ Heat 2–3 tablespoons groundnut oil in a wok or a large, deep skillet until very hot. Add the onions and stir-fry for about 2 minutes until beginning to soften. Add the garlic and ginger and stir-fry for another minute. Add the ham strips and stir to combine.

❷ Stir the cold cooked rice into the vegetables and ham mixture, then stir in the shrimp and the water chestnuts. Stir in 2 tablespoons of water and quickly cover the pan. Continue to cook for 2 minutes to heat the rice through, shaking the pan occasionally to prevent sticking.

❸ Beat the eggs with 1 teaspoon of the sesame oil, and season with salt and pepper. Make a well in the center of the rice mixture, add the eggs, and stir immediately, gradually drawing the rice into the eggs.

❹ Stir in the scallions, soy, and chili sauce, and stir-fry; stir in a little more water if the rice looks dry or is sticking. Drizzle in the remaining sesame oil and stir. Season to taste with salt and pepper.

❺ Remove from the heat, wipe the edge of the wok or skillet, and sprinkle the cilantro over the cooked rice. Serve immediately from the pan.

 easy

 serves 4–6

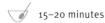 15–20 minutes

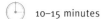 10–15 minutes

Singapore Noodles

2 oz/55 g dried Chinese
mushrooms
8 oz/225 g rice noodles
2–3 tbsp groundnut oil
6–8 garlic cloves, sliced
2–3 shallots, sliced thinly
1 inch/2.5 cm fresh ginger
root, peeled and sliced
4–5 red chiles, deseeded
and sliced diagonally
8 oz/225 g chicken
breast meat, sliced
8 oz/225 g snow peas,
sliced diagonally
8 oz/225 g bok choy,
shredded thinly
8 oz/225 g cooked
peeled shrimp
6–8 water chestnuts,
sliced
2 scallions, sliced thinly
2 tbsp chopped fresh
cilantro or mint

CURRY SAUCE
2 tbsp rice wine
2 tbsp soy sauce
3 tbsp medium or hot
Madras curry powder
1 tbsp sugar
1⅔ cups canned
coconut milk
salt and black pepper

 very easy

 serves 4–6

20 minutes,
plus 15 minutes
to soak

 9–10 minutes

❶ To make the curry sauce, whisk the rice wine and soy sauce into the curry powder, then stir in the sugar and the canned coconut milk, and season to taste with salt and black pepper.

❷ Put the Chinese mushrooms in a small bowl and add enough boiling water to cover them. Soak for about 15 minutes until softened. Lift out and squeeze out the liquid. Discard any stems, then slice thinly and set aside. Soak the rice noodles according to the instructions on the package, then drain well.

❸ Heat the oil in a wok or a deep skillet over a medium—high heat. Add the thinly sliced garlic, shallots, ginger, and chilesm and stir-fry for about 30 seconds. Add the chicken slices and the snow peas, and stir-fry for about 2 minutes. Add the bok choy, shrimp, water chestnuts, mushrooms, and scallions, and stir-fry for 1–2 minutes. Then add the curry sauce and noodles to the wok or skillet, stir-fry for 5 minutes, sprinkle with the cilantro, and serve.

Desserts

To finish off your hot and spicy lunch or evening meal with a sizzling dessert, this section gives a few ideas. Cool, exotic fruits taste cooler and jazzier when prepared with fresh ginger or dressed with a cardamom-flavored syrup. Lychee & Ginger Sorbet looks wonderful topped with slices of starfruit and slivers of preserved ginger, while the light and delicious Steamed Coconut Cake with Lime & Ginger makes a fitting end to a Thai-style feast.

Exotic Fruit Salad

INGREDIENTS

1 tsp jasmine tea
1 tsp grated fresh ginger
   root
1 strip lime zest
$\frac{1}{2}$ cup boiling water
2 tbsp superfine sugar
1 papaya
1 mango
$\frac{1}{2}$ small pineapple
1 starfruit
2 passionfruit

 extremely easy

serves 6

30 minutes,
plus 1 hour
to chill

0 minutes

❶ Place the tea, ginger, and lime zest in a heatproof cup, and pour the boiling water over them. Leave to infuse for 5 minutes, then strain the liquid.

❷ Add the sugar to the liquid and stir well to dissolve. Let the syrup cool completely.

❸ Halve, deseed, and peel the papaya. Halve the mango, remove the pit, and peel the fruit. Peel and remove the core from the pineapple. Cut the fruits into bite-sized pieces.

❹ Slice the starfruit crosswise. Place all the prepared fruits in a wide serving bowl and pour the cooled syrup over them. Cover with plastic wrap and chill for about 1 hour.

❺ Cut the passion-fruit in half, scoop out the flesh and mix it with the lime juice. Spoon over the salad and serve.

❸  ❹  ❺

COOK'S TIP
As they ripen and turn yellow, starfruit become delicately sweet and fragrant, but by then the tips of the ridges have turned brown, and you need to remove them before slicing. The easiest and quickest method of doing this is to run a vegetable peeler along each ridge.

Lychee & Ginger Sorbet

INGREDIENTS

14 oz/400 g cans
    lychees in syrup
finely grated zest of 1
    lime
2 tbsp lime juice
3 tbsp candied ginger
    syrup
2 egg whites

TO DECORATE
starfruit slices
slivers of candied ginger

very easy

serves 4

15–20 minutes,
plus 2½ hours
to freeze

0 minutes

❶ Drain the lychees, reserving the syrup. Place the fruits in a blender or a food processor with the lime zest, juice, and candied ginger syrup, and purée until completely smooth.

❷ Mix the purée thoroughly with the reserved lychee syrup, and pour the mixture into a freezerproof container and freeze for 1–1½ hours until the sorbet is slushy in texture. (Alternatively, use an ice-cream maker.)

❸ Remove from the freezer and whisk to break up the ice crystals. Whisk the egg whites in a clean, dry bowl until stiff, then fold in the iced mixture quickly and lightly.

❹ Return to the freezer and freeze until firm. Serve the sorbet in scoops, decorated with slices of starfruit and candied ginger.

❶  ❷  ❸

COOK'S TIP
It is not recommended that raw egg whites are served to very young children, pregnant women, the elderly or anyone weakened by chronic illness. The egg whites may be left out of this recipe, but you will need to whisk the sorbet a second time after another hour of freezing to obtain a light texture.

Pineapple with Cardamom & Lime

INGREDIENTS

1 pineapple
2 cardamom pods
1 thinly pared strip lime
   rind
1 tbsp soft light brown
   sugar
3 tbsp lime juice

❶ Cut the top and base from the pineapple, cut away the peel and remove the "eyes", then cut into quarters and remove the core, and slice lengthwise (see Cook's Tip).

❷ Crush the cardamom pods in a mortar and pestle and place in a pan with the lime rind and 4 tablespoons water. Heat until boiling, then simmer for 30 seconds. Remove from the heat and add the sugar, then cover and leave to infuse for 5 minutes.

❸ Stir in the sugar to dissolve, add the lime juice, then strain the syrup over the pineapple. Chill for 30 minutes.

❹ Arrange the pineapple on a serving dish, spoon over the syrup and serve.

easy

serves 4

15 minutes, plus 5
minutes to infuse,
30 minutes to chill

2–3 minutes

COOK'S TIP

To remove the eyes from pineapple, cut off the peel with a small, sharp knife to cut a V-shaped channel downward, cutting diagonally through the lines of brown eyes in the flesh, to make spiraling cuts round the fruit.

Steamed Coconut Cake with Lime & Ginger

INGREDIENTS

2 large eggs, separated
pinch of salt
$\frac{1}{2}$ cup superfine sugar
5 tbsp butter, melted
    and cooled
5 tbsp coconut milk
1 cups self-rising flour
$\frac{1}{2}$ tsp baking powder
3 tbsp shredded
    coconut
4 tbs candied ginger
    syrup
3 tbsp lime juice

TO DECORATE

3 pieces candied ginger
curls of grated fresh
    coconut

❶ Cut an 11 inch/27.5 cm round of nonstick paper and press into a 7 inch/17.5 cm steamer basket to line it.

❷ Whisk the egg whites with the salt until stiff. Gradually whisk in the sugar 1 tablespoon at a time, whisking hard after each addition until the mixture stands in stiff peaks.

❸ Whisk in the yolks, then quickly stir in the butter and coconut milk. Sift the flour and baking powder over the mixture, then fold in lightly and evenly with a large metal spoon. Fold in the coconut.

❹ Spoon the mixture into the lined steamer basket and tuck the spare paper over the top. Place the basket over boiling water, cover, and steam for 30 minutes.

❺ Turn out the cake onto a plate, remove the paper, and cool slightly. Mix together the ginger and lime juice and spoon over the cake. Cut it into squares and decorate them with diced candied ginger and curls of fresh coconut.

 very easy

 serves 8

15–20 minutes

30 minutes

INDEX